THE MASON JAR SCIENTIST

30 JARRING STEAM-BASED PROJECTS

BRENDA PRIDDY

FOR
YOUNG
READERS

Racehorse for Young Readers™ books may be purchased in bulk at special discounts for sales promotion, corporate gifts, fund-raising, or educational purposes. Special editions can also be created to specifications. For details, contact the Special Sales Department, Skyhorse Publishing, 307 West 36th Street, 11th Floor, New York, NY 10018 or info@skyhorsepublishing.com.

Racehorse for Young Readers™ is a pending trademark of Skyhorse Publishing, Inc.®, a Delaware corporation.

Visit our website at www.skyhorsepublishing.com.

10 9 8 7 6 5 4 3

Library of Congress Cataloging-in-Publication Data is available on file.

Cover photograph by Brenda Priddy
Cover design by Michael Short

ISBN: 978-1-6315-8311-7
Ebook ISBN: 978-1-6315-8320-9

Printed in China

TABLE OF CONTENTS

INTRODUCTION FOR PARENTS AND CAREGIVERS

A love of science is born at home.

For many kids, "why" is their favorite word. Science is all about answering the whys of the world.

The basis of scientific understanding is a natural part of a child's world. Watch a child play. You'll seen them question, test, analyze, and question again.

If you're a regular parent, grandparent, or caregiver, you may be wondering how you can help develop a love for science in the children under your care. Few of us have degrees in biochemistry or rocket science, but you don't have to be a professional scientist to encourage your children to understand their world.

All you need to become a scientist is a question and a jar.

So, gather your Mason jars, browse through this book, pick a question to answer, and have fun exploring the world of science, all within the confines of a jar.

You may be surprised at just how much your kids can learn in a jar!

The information and activities in this book are written for kids, so even if you can't be there to do every experiment, they can still explore and learn from each activity.

TIPS FOR SUCCESS

For best results, follow all steps exactly, paying special attention to measurements and times listed. Although science experiments are about exploring and being creative, precision is also important.

Take some time to discuss the science behind each of the experiments listed. You can use these activities as science demonstrations by following the steps exactly as listed. Or, use the STEAM extension ideas to expand on each idea and turn them into a complete STEAM activity.

Remember, any science experiment should include the following elements:

Question
Research
Hypothesis (what the child thinks may be the answer)
Experiment
Analyze the results and re-test if necessary
Form a conclusion

You don't have to be formal about these steps, but it's good to keep the information in the back of your mind as you go through the experiments with your kids. And if your kids get ahead of you and want to do the experiments without reading any of the science background, that's OK too!

What You Will Need

Although Mason jars are used in this book for every project, you can use any jar from your kitchen. Pickle jars, mayonnaise jars, jelly jars, or any other kind of plastic or glass jar will work just as well. The only thing you need to be a scientist is a jar!

Before starting each project, make sure you have all the necessary supplies. You'll also want to have a pair of safety goggles to protect your eyes when completing these projects.

Disclaimer

Adult supervision is recommended for the projects in this book. Please read the instructions for each activity before deciding if the activity is appropriate for the children or child who will be doing the activity. Follow all safety precautions before completing any of the activities listed here.

SECTION 1: WEATHER

What is weather?

Where does wind come from?

What are clouds?

Why does it rain?

You probably have a lot of questions about how weather works. Adults who study the weather are called meteorologists. Meteorologists track weather patterns and study the atmosphere. This helps us learn about weather that is coming, and what causes it. And it helps us figure out what to wear each day.

You can become a meteorologist in your own backyard with these weather science experiments.

How Do Clouds Form?

Do you know what a cloud is?

A cloud is a group of ice and water particles suspended together in the atmosphere.

Gravity brings these water and ice particles together. Scientists call this *water vapor*. The weight of the cloud of water vapor brings it closer to the ground where it is warmer. When a lot of the cloud melts, it falls to the ground as rain.

You don't have to travel to space to experience a cloud first-hand. Follow the directions below and you'll soon have your very own cloud in a jar!

Gather your supplies:

- Black or blue paper
- Mason jar
- Water
- Blue food coloring
- Hairspray
- Ice
- Small bowl

Tape your paper behind your jar. You don't have to use an extra piece of paper, but the cloud is easier to see if you tape a piece of dark paper behind it.

Fill your bowl with ice.

Fill your jar 1/3 of the way full with water. Add a drop of blue food coloring and stir.

Heat your water in the microwave for about 20 seconds. You want the water to be about 120 degrees for the best cloud.

Spray the surface of the water with hairspray, then quickly place the bowl of ice on top of the jar.

Wait a few seconds, and you'll see the cloud start to form.

Pro tip: Spray the hairspray directly into the center of the water and not the sides of the jar. If you spray the jar, you won't be able to see the cloud.

The Science

The air contains a lot of moisture.

When water evaporates, it turns into water vapor and is carried into the atmosphere. As the water vapor climbs higher, it starts to freeze.

The cooler air causes the water droplets to stick

to ice, sea salt, and dust, creating a visible cloud.

In this experiment, the hairspray acts like the dust that clouds cling to in nature. The hairspray helps the vapor particles stick together just like a real cloud.

Questions to Ask

What happens to the cloud if you don't use hairspray?

Will other aerosol sprays make better clouds?

If you use a bigger container, will the cloud be bigger?

Does the amount of ice in the bowl affect the cloud's visibility?

STEAM Extensions

Science: Add other cold things to the bowl, like cold water, ice cream, or frozen peas. What makes the best cloud?

Technology: Film the cloud as you remove the bowl from the top of the jar. Play back the video in slow motion. Where does the cloud go?

Engineering: How are the other cloud types formed? Can you make them in your jar?

Art: Draw a picture of the most common cloud shapes. What kind did you make in the jar?

Math: How long does it take for the cloud to form? How long does it take to dissipate? How cold does the water have to be to make a cloud?

HOW IS FROST MADE?

Have you ever scratched the frost off a cold window? Maybe you've touched the frost that forms on freezers in the grocery store.

We see frost almost every day during the winter, but have you ever thought about how frost is made?

Frost is like snow, but thanks to condensation, frost appears even when it's not snowing. Follow along with these steps to make your own frost in a jar. You'll learn what frost is and why it appears.

Gather your supplies:

- Mason jar
- Mason jar lid
- Ice
- Water
- Blue food coloring
- Salt

Fill your jar with ice. Pour a tablespoon of water over your ice. Add a drop of blue food coloring to make your frost stand out.

Sprinkle salt over the ice and close the jar.

Shake the jar vigorously for about 60 seconds.

Set the jar on the counter and watch what happens. Frost will already cling to the sides of the jar.

After about five minutes, there will be a thick layer of frost on your jar.

Scratch the jar with your fingernail. It's super cold!

The Science

Our air contains a lot more water than we realize. Water particles in the air are called *water vapor*. Water can be a liquid, a solid, or a gas. Water vapor is water's gaseous state.

When one side of a surface has a much lower temperature than the other side, water vapor changes into liquid on the higher-temperature side. This causes condensation on the surface.

When one side of the jar is below freezing, instead of turning into condensation, the water vapor turns into frost.

Adding salt lowers the melting point of ice and causes the entire surface of the jar to drop below freezing. This helps your frost form faster.

Questions to Ask

Does adding more water make a difference in how fast your frost forms?

Does adding more salt make the frost appear faster or slower?

What happens when the jar is filled mostly with water?

STEAM Extensions

Science: Experiment with using different amounts of water, ice, and salt in the jar. Which mixture creates the thickest layer of frost? Which mixture freezes fastest?

Technology: Examine the frost with a magnifying glass. What patterns do you see in the frost?

Art: Scratch designs onto the outside of your jar with a toothpick.

Engineering: Try making frost in other containers, such as plastic, metal, or cloth. Which container produces frost the fastest?

Math: Calculate how long it takes for frost to form. How long does the temperature in the jar stay below freezing?

WHY IS THE SKY BLUE?

You know the sky is blue. Even a very young child will draw a picture with blue sky and green grass.

But have you ever thought about *why* the sky is blue? Why doesn't the sky look purple or green?

The secret is in our atmosphere, and the round shape of the earth. Complete this experiment and see for yourself why the sky looks blue.

Gather your supplies:

- Mason jar
- Water
- Milk
- Black paper
- Flashlight

Fill your jar with water and add about a tablespoon of milk to make the water cloudy.

Tape a piece of black paper behind your jar and turn out the lights.

Shine a flashlight through the jar. The water will appear blue!

Pro tip: **The darker your room, the bluer your water will appear.**

The Science

The light we see from the sun looks white, but it contains all the colors of the rainbow (red, orange, yellow, green, blue, and purple). This is the visible light spectrum of the human eye.

Light travels in waves. Each color of light travels at a different wavelength. Red light has the longest waves and blue light has the shortest waves.

When light from the sun enters the atmosphere, the light hits particles in the air and the light waves are scattered. Blue light has the shortest waves, so it is scattered the most. When we look at the sky, we see the blue light reflected from all of the millions of particles in the air.

The same thing happens in your jar. The milk takes the place of air particles. When you shine the white flashlight on the side of the jar, all you see is the reflected blue light.

Questions to Ask

What happens when you shine other colors of light on the jar?

Does changing the angle of the flashlight change colors?

Why doesn't the water look blue when you look at it in a bright room?

STEAM Extensions

Science: Learn about the visible light spectrum and how light travels in waves.

Technology: Use a prism to reflect a sunray. A prism separates all the colors of light and reflects their true colors.

Engineering: Does changing the size or shape of the jar or the type of flashlight change your results? Can you get the jar to glow green, red, or yellow?

Art: Draw the results of your experiment.

Math: Research the wavelengths of the visible light spectrum. Is there light that we can't see with human eyes?

HOW DO TORNADOES WORK?

A tornado is a powerful and destructive wind funnel. Tornadoes are one of Earth's deadliest natural disasters. Some tornadoes can travel up to 300 miles per hour and destroy entire towns.

A tornado forms when warm air mixes with cold air. If the air meets in just the right way, it creates a vertical column of rotating air known as a funnel cloud or vortex. If the funnel cloud reaches the ground, that's a tornado.

Although real tornados are incredibly dangerous, you can safely learn how tornados form when you make your own tornado in a jar!

Gather your supplies:

- Mason jar
- Mason jar lid
- Water
- Food coloring
- Dish soap
- Glitter
- Dark paper

Fill your jar with water. Add a drop of food coloring to the water but keep it light. The darker the water, the harder it is to see your tornado.

Drop a small dab of dish soap and a small sprinkle of glitter to the jar. Seal the jar tightly.

Shake the jar using a circular motion. Place it in front of your dark paper to see it better. The vortex will appear in the center of the jar.

Pro tip: If your jar gets full of bubbles, let it sit for a while before spinning it. Too many bubbles cloud the water and you won't be able to see your tornado.

The Science

Spinning a jar forms a vortex in the center of the jar.

Tornadoes are formed by vortexes in weather patterns. When a patch of cold air hits a patch of warm air in a circular motion, a tornado can form.

Just like in the jar, the vortex starts high in the sky but descends to the ground like a funnel. When the tornado touches down, the power of the wind destroys everything in its path.

Questions to Ask

Is there a way to stop tornadoes from forming?

What makes some areas prone to tornadoes?

How many tornadoes are formed each year?

STEAM Extensions

Science: Can you get a better tornado to form in differently-shaped containers? Does the temperature of the water affect how the tornado forms?

Technology: Research the weather patterns from your area over the last year. How do meteorologists watch out for tornadoes? How do they predict where they will go?

Engineering: Research what steps building manufacturers take to make their buildings tornado-proof. What materials are used to minimize tornado damage?

Art: Place a piece of paper inside an empty jar. Place a marble in the jar along with a drop of paint. Spin the jar using a circular motion. Take out the paper. You've created a tornado painting!

Math: How many tornadoes affect your area in a year? What is the cost of tornado damage in your city or country?

WHY DOES RAIN FALL?

Rain is an important part of our world. Without rain, all living things on earth would die.

But have you ever considered why it rains?

What makes water that's in the sky fall back to earth?

This simple experiment illustrates why rain falls. All you need is some shaving cream, food coloring, and a jar!

Gather your supplies:

- Mason jar
- Water
- Shaving cream
- Small cup or bowl
- Food coloring
- Pipette

Fill your jar about 2/3 of the way full of water. Add a layer of shaving cream to the top of the jar. This represents the cloud.

Fill a small cup or bowl with water and add a few drops of food coloring.

Use a pipette to drop this colored water onto the shaving-cream cloud.

After a while, the colored water becomes too heavy for the cloud and it falls into the water below.

Pro tip: The thicker your cloud, the longer it will take for the colored water to break through the cloud. If you find you're waiting a long time without any rain falling into your jar, start over with a thinner cloud.

The Science

Clouds are made up of a mixture of water vapor, ice, and particles such as dust and gas. Gravity pulls these materials together.

Over time, the clouds become heavier and heavier. When the cloud is too heavy for the atmosphere, the cloud sinks. As it enters warmer air, the ice in the cloud starts to melt and the water falls back to earth as rain.

Questions to Ask

Are some clouds more prone to rain than others?

How does rain affect the shape of clouds?

Are there some clouds that never rain?

STEAM Extensions

Science: Learn about the water cycle. Why is rain an important part of the water cycle?

Technology: Find out how meteorologists track cloud patterns and use this data to estimate the upcoming weather for the area.

Engineering: What steps do engineers and designers take to make sure clouds won't damage airplanes and other aerial objects?

Art: Instead of doing this activity in a jar, make it into an art painting! Lay a piece of paper in a plastic tray. Place a mesh colander over the paper flipped upside down, making a cage. Spray shaving cream onto the colander to make the cloud, then squeeze the colored water onto the cloud and let it drip onto the paper to make a rain painting.

Math: Find out how much a typical cloud weighs. Do all types of clouds weigh the same? How heavy does a cloud have to be before it rains?

WHAT IS THE GREENHOUSE EFFECT?

A greenhouse is a building made entirely of glass. Greenhouses are used to grow plants when it's too cold to grow them outside.

A greenhouse works because sunlight and heat can enter the building through the glass, but the heat gets trapped under the glass and can't escape. This means that the inside of the building is hotter than it is outside the glass.

Our atmosphere acts like a greenhouse for the earth. Gases in the atmosphere allow heat and light through, but don't allow it back out.

This warms the earth and protects it from sudden temperature drops once the sun goes down.

Watch the greenhouse effect in action with this simple experiment.

Gather your supplies:

- 3 mason jars
- 2 mason jar lids
- Water
- 3 thermometers

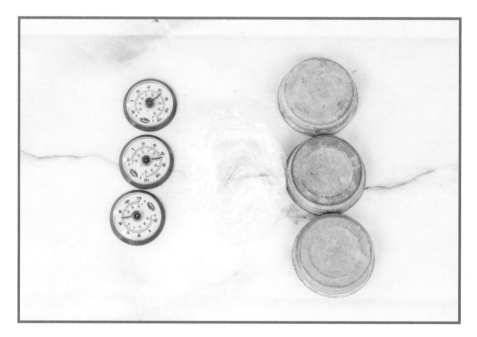

- Plastic baggie
- Plastic wrap

Wrap one of your thermometers in the plastic baggie to keep it from getting damaged in the water.

Fill one jar with water and put the wrapped thermometer inside. Place a piece of plastic wrap over the top of the jar and screw on the lid.

Place another thermometer inside a dry jar and cover with plastic wrap. Seal the jar closed with a lid.

In the last jar, put the thermometer in, but don't seal the jar.

Place the jars in a sunny location. Record the starting temperature of the jars.

Pro tip: Find inexpensive thermometers at a pet store in the reptile section.

Wait three hours. Examine the current temperature inside each

jar and record your results. Which jar got the warmest? Which was the coldest?

The Science

Without the greenhouse effect, Earth would quickly become a giant ice ball.

The atmosphere traps the heat from the sun and keeps it near the surface of the planet. Without greenhouse gases, the earth cannot retain heat efficiently. Without greenhouse gases, the temperature on earth would fall to about zero degrees Fahrenheit.

Without the atmosphere and the greenhouse effect, the Earth could not sustain life as we know it.

Questions to Ask

Can the greenhouse effect ever be bad?

What happens when there are holes in the atmosphere?

Do other planets in our solar system have an atmosphere?

STEAM Extensions

Science: What would happen if the earth's average temperature fell by 10 degrees? What if it rose by 10 degrees?

Technology: How do scientists keep an eye on our atmosphere to ensure we don't damage it beyond repair?

Engineering: How does the greenhouse effect change how buildings are made? Is the greenhouse effect considered when choosing materials for a building?

Art: Draw your vision of how the atmosphere protects the earth.

Math: How do meteorologists track the greenhouse effect? How is this data used to benefit humans?

SECTION 2: CHEMICAL REACTIONS

Fizz, pop, bang!

We all love flashy, explosive science experiments.

But do you know what type of science causes these flashy results?

Most flashy science experiments are the result of chemical reactions. When materials with different properties mix, they sometimes cause a reaction, ending in an explosion or eruption.

In a chemical reaction, the bonds between molecules break and re-combine to create new molecules.

Questions about what kind of molecules are involved, what sort of interactions they create, and what happens keep many scientists busy. A scientist who studies chemicals and reactions is a chemist.

You can become a chemist at home when you complete these chemical reaction experiments!

HOW DO POLYMER CHAINS WORK?

You've seen stretchy slime. It's fun to pull and squish slime between your fingers.

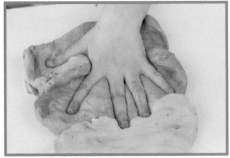

But did you know that when you play with slime, you are playing with a chemical reaction?

Slime is created from polymer chains, which are repeating chains of linked molecules called monomers. These polymer chains are created when the boron in the laundry starch mixes with the polyvinyl acetate in the glue. This process is called polymerization.

Become an at-home chemist when you make this version of fluffy slime.

Gather your supplies:

- Mason jar
- Elmer's clear glue
- White shaving cream
- Food coloring
- Sta-flo laundry starch

Mix 1-part glue with 2-parts shaving cream in your jar. Add your food coloring and stir.

Measure 1 part of starch and set aside. Add the starch to the glue mixture a tablespoon at a time. Stir after each addition. You may not need to use all of the starch. Once the mixture starts clinging to your spoon, it's ready to remove from the container.

At this point, the slime will still be sticky, but keep stretching the slime to complete the bonding process, which will remove the stickiness.

If you have stretched the slime for over thirty seconds and it is still sticky, add a little bit more starch to the slime.

Pro tip: If your slime is too stringy, you may have added too much starch. Run the mixture under cool water for a few seconds and the stringy slime will solidify.

The Science

When the molecules in the starch and the glue react, they form long polymer chains that lie side by side. The molecules can slide past one another, which keeps the slime stretchy. The longer the polymer chain, the stronger the bond.

Adding shaving cream to your slime introduces air into the mixture. This makes the slime fluffy and squishy.

Questions to Ask

Can you make slime using other materials?

What happens when you add other ingredients to the glue mixture?

How does the brand of materials change the strength of the slime?

STEAM Extensions

Science: Experiment with other slime recipes. Try using baking soda, dish soap, magnesium flakes, contact solution, and borax as your activators. How does the slime change?

Technology: Examine your materials under a microscope before mixing. After mixing, examine the slime. How have the materials changed?

Engineering: When would an engineer need to use a flexible material? How do you think mechanical engineers balance the need for strong materials versus flexible materials?

Art: Make different colors of slime and share with friends. Our version is a fluffy sunset slime.

Math: Change the amount of glue, starch, or shaving cream used in your slime recipes. How does the mixture change?

WHAT IS AN ENDOTHERMIC REACTION?

Did you know that there are two types of chemical reactions?

A chemical reaction can either make energy or use energy.

Chemical reactions that use energy are called endothermic reactions. Reactions that make energy are called exothermic reactions.

You can tell if a reaction is endothermic or exothermic because the products will either be cooler or warmer after reacting.

An endothermic reaction is cooler after reacting. An exothermic reaction is warmer after reacting.

You might not know it, but the classic volcano science experiment is an example of an endothermic reaction.

Try it out for yourself using these steps!

Gather your supplies:

- 6 mason jars
- Vinegar
- Food coloring (optional)
- Dish soap
- Thermometer
- Baking soda

Fill your jars with ½ a cup of vinegar each. Dye the liquid in each jar a different color.

Add a squeeze of dish soap to each of the jars.

Pro tip: Place a large tray under your jars to catch the drips.

Place a thermometer in each of the jars and record the starting temperature.

Drop baking soda into each of the jars and watch as the chemicals react.

Test the temperature inside the jars after the reaction has occurred. How much cooler are the materials now?

The Science

A chemical reaction consists of two or more reactants that react to create a new product. During the reaction, existing molecular bonds are broken down and new bonds are formed, resulting in the new product

Baking soda is a base and vinegar is an acid, and their reaction produces gas. This classic reaction absorbs energy, making it an endothermic reaction.

When energy is absorbed, the temperature of the remaining mixture is reduced by several degrees.

Questions to Ask

What happens when you use warm vinegar rather than cold?

Will using other acids, such as lemon juice, cause the same results?

Does the temperature get even lower if you use more of the materials?

STEAM Extensions

Science: Try this experiment with other acids and bases and record the results. Are all acid and base reactions endothermic?

Technology: Create a presentation of your results and share it with family or your class at school.

Engineering: Try this experiment in other types of containers. Does the shape affect the results at all?

Art: Make a rainbow of color when completing this experiment for spectacular results.

Math: How much does the temperature drop after the reaction occurs? How long does it take before the temperature normalizes?

WILL OIL AND WATER MIX?

Oil and water don't mix. This is so well-known that an expression for things that don't mix well is, "They go together like oil and water."

But what if there was a way to get oil and water to mix?

Try this experiment to see if you can get the classic enemies of oil and water to get along together.

Gather your supplies:

- Mason jar
- Mason jar lid
- Water
- Food coloring
- Oil
- Egg

Fill your jar half full of water. Place a few drops of your favorite food coloring into the jar.

Fill the rest of the jar up with oil.

Close the lid tightly, and shake.

After a few seconds, the oil and water will separate.

Open the lid and crack open an egg. Add the egg to the jar and close the lid.

Shake the jar vigorously.

Set the jar down and watch what happens. The oil and water stay mixed!

The Science

While oil and water are not attracted to each other, the molecules in the egg are attracted to both oil and water molecules.

When you shake up the jar and mix the egg molecules in with the water and oil, the egg molecules bond with both the water and the oil molecules. This process is called emulsion. An emulsifier (the egg) allows molecules to bond that are ordinarily not able to mix.

Questions to Ask

What other additives might cause oil and water to bond?

How much egg do you have to add to make oil and water mix?

What happens if the oil and water are hot?

STEAM Extensions

Science: Try other additives to see if they make oil and water mix. Try sugar, butter, detergent, hair gel, and body wash.

Technology: Research emulsifiers in food. What are the most common emulsifiers?

Engineering: How do emulsifiers improve the shelf life of food?

Art: Draw the results of your experiment.

Math: How much of each emulsifier do you have to add to get the experiment to work?

HOW IS BUTTER MADE?

Nothing is more delicious than butter spread onto a warm roll fresh out of the oven. But did you know that the process of making butter is a chemical reaction?

Without chemical reactions, we wouldn't have delicious butter for making cookies and spreading on toast.

The secret to making butter is agitation.

Learn how to make your own butter in this fun experiment.

Gather your supplies:

- Whipping cream
- Mason jar
- Mason jar lid

Bring your cream to room temperature.

Fill your jar half way with cream.

Screw the lid onto your jar tightly.

Shake!

Within a few minutes, the cream will start to thicken. Keep shaking!

After a while, the cream will turn into clumpy curds. You're not done yet!

Shake the jar until a solid lump of butter forms and the buttermilk separates from the butter.

The Science

Butter is formed when cream is agitated (shaken). This causes the fat molecules to fly out of place and cling together, eventually separating completely from the liquid in the cream.

The leftover liquid is what we call buttermilk.

Questions to Ask

Does the temperature of the cream change how the butter forms?

Can you make butter from milk?

Does using whipping cream versus heavy whipping cream make a difference in butter formation?

STEAM Extensions

Science: Try making butter with cold cream and with warm cream. Which butter is ready first?

Technology: Research how butter is made. How has butter making changed over the centuries?

Engineering: Try making butter in differently shaped containers. Which produces butter the fastest?

Art: Many artists use butter to make sculptures. After making your butter, see what you can shape it into.

Math: What is the ideal temperature for making butter? Does the amount of cream added to the jar affect how long it takes to turn into butter?

CAN WE SEE CARBON DIOXIDE?

Did you know that gases have different weights?

Air is made up of several gases, including nitrogen, carbon dioxide, oxygen, and helium. Some of these gases are lighter than air.

In this science experiment, you will learn how to make a reaction that produces carbon dioxide, and see if it's heavier or lighter than air.

Gather your supplies:

- Mason jar
- Water
- Food coloring
- Baby oil
- Alka-Seltzer tablets

Fill your mason jar with one inch of water.

Add a few drops of food coloring to your water and stir.

Fill the rest of the jar with oil.

Break an Alka-Seltzer tablet into small pieces.

Drop the pieces one by one into the jar and watch what happens. The colored water will move to the top of the jar just like a lava lamp!

The Science

Why does adding Alka-Seltzer tablets to the water make it bubble and boil?

The secret is the chemical reaction.

Alka-Seltzer tablets contain dehydrated citric acid and sodium bicarbonate. These two chemicals react when the tablets hit the water, creating a byproduct of carbon dioxide gas.

Carbon dioxide is lighter than the water and oil in the jar, so it travels to the surface of the jar. Some of the colored liquid sticks to these particles of gas, which are carried to the top of the jar and released once the gas escapes the jar.

This makes the liquid inside the jar look like a lava lamp.

Questions to Ask

Can anything else make the water boil?

Does adding more oil make a difference in how the reaction occurs?

How is carbon dioxide made?

STEAM Extensions

Science: Learn about carbon dioxide. What is it used for? Is it always good or can it be harmful?

Technology: Research the chemical formula of carbon dioxide, sodium bicarbonate, citric acid, water, and oil.

Engineering: Experiment with using different ratios of water and oil in the jar. Does this change the reaction? What if you use another liquid instead of water?

Art: Make a 3D model of the chemical formula for carbon dioxide from modeling clay.

Math: How long does the reaction last? Will changing the temperature of the water or oil change the reaction time?

WHAT IS AN EXOTHERMIC REACTION?

Chemical reactions can either make energy or use energy.

An endothermic reaction uses energy, but an exothermic reaction creates energy.

Exothermic reactions occur in a lot of familiar places, such as a car engine, stove, compost, and even your own human body.

Exothermic reactions create heat energy that can be re-purposed for other tasks.

This experiment mixes yeast and hydrogen peroxide to make an exothermic reaction that you can safely feel.

Gather your supplies:

- Mason jar
- Food coloring
- Dry yeast packets
- Warm water
- Dish soap
- 6% hydrogen peroxide

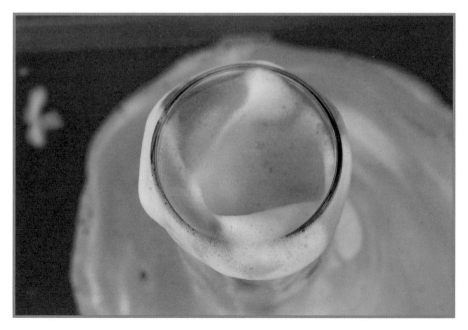

Coat the inside of your jar with streaks of food coloring.

Mix the yeast packet with ¼ of a cup of warm water in a separate container. Let the yeast sit for about 2 minutes.

Add a few drops of dish soap to the yeast and pour the liquid into your mason jar

Slowly pour hydrogen peroxide into the jar. The two liquids will react and expand, rising to the top of the jar.

Keep adding hydrogen peroxide to the jar until the yeast no longer reacts.

Touch the foam—it's warm to the touch!

The Science

Hydrogen peroxide breaks down over time into water and oxygen. When you add the yeast to the mixture, hydrogen peroxide breaks down a lot faster.

This causes the hydrogen peroxide to release oxygen quickly, which rises into the air.

The yeast and dish soap get caught up with the oxygen, creating a tower of warm foam.

Questions to Ask

Why do some reactions make energy, and some use it?

Does changing the temperature of the yeast mixture affect the reaction?

How could this reaction be used in real life?

STEAM Extensions

Science: Experiment with using different types of yeast and different strengths of hydrogen peroxide. What mixture creates the best reaction?

Technology: Find out how exothermic reactions are used in real life.

Engineering: Try this experiment in differently shaped containers. How does the shape of the container affect how the mixture reacts?

Art: After your reaction occurs, place a piece of cardstock paper over the foam. Lift the foam and let the paper dry. You'll be left with a colorful bubble pattern on your paper.

Math: Calculate how long the reaction occurs with each variable. Use a thermometer to check the temperature of the ingredients before and after the reaction to see how much energy is released.

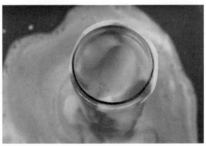

SECTION 3: PLANTS AND BIOMES

Biology is more than just plants. Of all the areas of science, biology has some of the most uses in our everyday lives.

Biologists use science to learn the best way to raise plants, how to improve the food we eat, and how to keep pests away.

Become a biologist and learn more about how plants and biomes work in this series of experiments.

You'll learn about capillary action, why biomes exist, how seeds sprout, how trees breathe, why the earth has layers, and how plants absorb water.

WHAT IS CAPILLARY ACTION?

Did you know that water is sticky?

Although it doesn't feel like it, water molecules like to stick together through a process known as cohesion. Cohesion helps water form into droplets and puddles. Water is friendly and wants to hang out with other water molecules.

The stickiness of water causes capillary action. Capillary action allows liquid to flow through narrow spaces in opposition to gravitational force.

Since water molecules like to stick together, they will adhere to the walls of just about anything.

In a small space, the pressure from the water molecules sticking to each other and to the walls of the space places an upward force on the liquid. When the bond to the walls of the space is stronger than the bond between individual water molecules, the water travels up.

Gravity and surface tension affect how far water will travel.

Because paper towels are so absorbent, they are the perfect tool to use to illustrate how capillary action works.

Gather your supplies:

- Paper towels
- Food coloring
- 6 mason jars

Fill three mason jars full of water. Dye one jar red, one jar blue, and one jar yellow.

Arrange your mason jars in a circle with an empty jar between each jar of colored water.

Drape a paper towel between each empty jar and the full jar next to it. Make sure the paper towel is touching the water. Each jar will have two paper towels in it.

Wait 24 hours.

Observe the liquid in the jars. The liquid from the first three jars will spread to the remaining three jars, creating green, purple, and orange-colored water.

Pro tip: Roll your paper towels into tubes and your water will travel faster.

The Science

There's a lot going on in this experiment. Capillary action works because multiple forces are in play.

Surface tension keeps the water traveling up the paper towels, while the absorbency of the paper towels keeps the liquid from falling to the table below, in direct opposition to gravity.

When the three colors from each of the jars spill into the empty jars, they combine to make secondary colors and complete the rainbow.

Capillary action is used in many natural processes and is one of the ways your body moves blood through your blood vessels. Plants, trees, towels, and fountain pens also use capillary action to function.

Questions to Ask

Will other materials work in place of the paper towels?

How would the earth look different if there were no capillary action?

Can you mix other colors this way?

STEAM Extensions

Science: Experiment with using other items to carry the liquid from one container to another. Try coffee filters, wool cloth, socks, and straw wrappers.

Technology: Research everyday items that use capillary action.

Engineering: Capillary action determines how ground water behaves in soil. Civil and environmental engineers must consider capillary action when building roads and other structures. How would capillary action affect structures made by humans?

Art: Learn about primary and secondary colors. Why are blue, yellow, and red primary colors?

Math: How long does it take for the liquids to even out between all the jars? Why does the liquid remain the same level in all the jars?

WHAT ARE BIOMES?

A biome is an area of the earth with a specific climate, types of plants, and animals. A biome can be made up of many ecosystems (usually very similar ones).

Common biomes include freshwater, marine, desert, tundra, grasslands, rainforest, and savannah.

Each of these biomes can be recreated in a jar, but this experiment focuses on desert, rainforest, and freshwater biomes.

Gather your supplies:

Desert Biome:
- Mason jar
- Mason jar lid
- Sand
- Potting soil
- Succulent plant
- Small rocks

Freshwater Biome:
- Mason jar
- Mason jar lid
- Sand
- Potting soil
- Freshwater plant
- Pebbles

Rainforest Biome:
- Mason jar
- Mason jar lid
- Potting soil
- Small plant (indoor plants work well)
- Small rocks

Fill each jar about halfway with the sand or soil. Add a bit of potting soil to the sand in the freshwater and desert biomes to give your plant nutrients as it grows.

Dig a small hole into the center of each jar and add your plant.

Add decorative rocks to each jar.

Add enough water to the rainforest and desert biomes to make the sand slightly damp and the soil damp but not wet.

Fill the freshwater jar with water.

Screw the lids onto each jar.

Place in a sunny location and keep an eye on them for several weeks. The plants will thrive in their new biomes!

The Science

Creatures and plants on the earth depend on one another. All living things are connected. Each living creature depends on millions of other living organisms to survive.

Organisms that need each other gather together. This collection of dependent organisms is called an ecosystem.

Biomes are simply large sections of the globe containing a lot of similar ecosystems. The earth contains many different biomes.

Questions to Ask

How long will your jar biomes last?

Would introducing small insects, worms, fish, or reptiles change your biomes?

Why are biomes important?

STEAM Extensions

Science: Research the major biomes in the world. What type of biome do you live in?

Technology: How do scientists use biomes to learn more about how the world works? Why is it important to identify biomes and ecosystems?

Engineering: How do engineers consider biomes when designing structures, cars, and other items? What role do biomes play in creating eco-friendly spaces?

Art: Draw a picture of your favorite biome.

Math: How can math be used to preserve biomes and ecosystems? What sort of statistical data could mathematicians use to learn more about biomes?

HOW DO SEEDS SPROUT?

Put a seed into the ground and a few weeks later, you'll see a tiny sprout that grows into a plant.

But have you ever considered how seeds sprout?

How does placing a seed into soil and giving it moisture create a new life?

Use this experiment to learn more about how and why seeds grow.

Gather your supplies:

- Mason jar
- Potting soil
- Water
- Fast-growing seeds
- Magnifying glass

Fill your jar about ¾ of the way full with potting soil.

Add enough water to make the soil damp.

Scatter the seeds across the surface of the soil. Add a tiny layer of soil over the seeds.

Place the jar in a sunny location and wait.

Within a few days, the seeds will break open and push out roots and leaves.

The Science

Dry seeds are dormant. This means that the seed is inactive and is not trying to grow. When seeds receive water, oxygen, and the right temperature, the seed will start the germination process. Light can also affect germination. Some seeds require light to germinate, while others require full darkness.

Seeds exposed to the right conditions take in water an oxygen through the seed coat. The seed absorbs the water and oxygen which enlarges the embryo's cells hidden under the seed coat. This breaks open the seed coat, and a radicle (root) emerges. Soon after, a plumule (the stem) emerges from the other side, bringing the leaves above the surface of the soil.

Questions to Ask

What makes a seed hardy or weak?

Why do some seeds have to lie dormant for months before sprouting?

What would happen if seeds no longer existed?

STEAM Extensions

Science: Make two jars of seeds. Place one in a sunny location and one in a dark location. Does this change what happens to the seeds?

Technology: Research how seeds are harvested and stored for crop planting.

Engineering: What makes plants grow better? What steps do farmers take to ensure their plants grow to their full potential? Are there any machines that help with growing plants?

Art: Trace the root patterns of your plants onto a piece of paper. It looks like beautiful art!

Math: Track how long it takes for your seeds to sprout. How long does it take for them to grow to their full size? How long does it take to make a flower or fruit?

HOW DO TREES BREATHE?

Trees are living organisms, just like people. In a way, trees "breathe" just like we do. Trees require a mixture of gases to live just like humans do.

But the way trees get their air is a bit different from humans. Trees use a process known as photosynthesis to take in the gases they need to survive.

Complete this experiment to watch a tree breathing in action and learn more about photosynthesis.

Gather your supplies:

- Leaves from plants or trees (freshly picked)
- Mason jars
- Water

Pull some fresh leaves off a variety of trees and plants.

Fill several mason jars with water.

Submerge the leaves inside the jars, some face up and some face down.

Wait several hours.

Examine the surface of the leaves. They are covered in tiny bubbles. The bubbles are the oxygen that the leaf is breathing out.

The Science

All plants require sunlight, water, and carbon dioxide to live. Opposite to humans, plants breathe in carbon dioxide and breathe out oxygen (during photosynthesis).

During photosynthesis, plants use a compound called chlorophyll in their leaves to capture sunlight.

Photosynthesis has two phases.

In phase one, the chloroplasts (where chlorophyll is stored) store energy from sunlight. The chloroplasts store the sun's energy in a chemical called ATP (adenosine triphosphate). In the second phase, ATP is converted into sugar and other organic compounds. This is the food that the plants actually "eat."

In the process of creating ATP, oxygen is given off as a byproduct, similar to how we breathe out carbon dioxide after using oxygen.

You can see the oxygen gather on the surface of the leaf under the water. The gas gets trapped under the water, forming bubbles. If you shake the jar, the bubbles will rise to the surface and enter the air.

Questions to Ask:

How to plants breathe at night?

Do all plants need sunlight?

How much oxygen does one tree produce?

STEAM Extensions

Science: Place one jar in a light area and one jar in the dark. Do the leaves produce different levels of oxygen?

Technology: Examine a leaf under a microscope. Can you see the chloroplasts?

Engineering: Plants require different levels of water, sunlight, and carbon dioxide. How would you use this information to plan a garden in your yard?

Art: Sandwich a leaf between two pieces of paper. Rub a crayon or piece of chalk over the leaf to make leaf rubbings.

Math: Find out how many trees it takes to make enough oxygen for a person to breathe.

HOW DO PLANTS DRINK?

Plants require carbon dioxide, sunlight, and water to grow.

But how do a plant's roots absorb water? How does water get from the roots to the leaves?

It's all thanks to a process known as osmosis.

Complete this osmosis experiment and watch the process in action.

Gather your supplies:

- Mason jar
- Blue food coloring
- Celery
- water

Fill your jar with water. Add several drops of blue food coloring to the water. You'll want the water to be quite dark.

Ask an adult to cut the bottom part of the celery off (this helps it absorb the water faster). Place the celery inside the jar.

Wait a few hours and watch what happens. The celery's stalk and leaves will start to turn blue.

The longer you leave the celery in the jar, the bluer the celery will become.

The Science

Plants can pull water from the soil thanks to a process called osmosis. Osmosis can be a bit confusing to understand, but you can think of it like this:

> In any solution, molecules make up the solvent (the larger part of a solution) and the solute (the smaller parts in a solution). The molecules in a solution like to be evenly spread, so they move around. If there are more solute particles in one area of the solution, they will move from that area to the area with less solute particles.

Fun fact: scientists didn't know that osmosis existed until the mid-twentieth century!

A plant's roots are designed to take advantage of osmosis. Roots are made up of hair-like particles that have a large surface area. The roots absorb the water from the surrounding soil, which causes them to fill with water and swell. The pressure of the swollen roots moves the water up by capillary action through tiny tubes in the plant (xylem) that go up to the plant's leaves.

When you use colored water, you can see the path that it travels through celery's xylem and leaves because they turn that color!

Questions to Ask

Does a plant with roots absorb more water than a plant with its roots cut off?

How long can a plant survive without its roots?

How long does it take for the celery stalk to turn green again when placed in clear water?

STEAM Extensions

Science: Try this experiment with plants with roots, plants that are roots (like a carrot), and the original cut-off celery. Which one absorbs more of the colored water?

Technology: Why do you think it took scientists so long to learn about osmosis? Are there still scientific mysteries today?

Engineering: How is osmosis used in human-produced machines and processes?

Art: Split your celery between two jars of water. Dye the water in each jar a different color. Is the color split on the leaves, or shared between the two sides of the plant?

Math: Calculate how long it takes for the colored water to reach the tip of the celery.

WHY DO ROCKS HAVE LAYERS?

Have you ever looked at a rock that's been cut open?

Many rocks have visible stripes and layers.

You may wonder why so many rocks have stripes.

The answer lies in how rocks are formed.

Complete this experiment to learn how rocks form, and what makes the layers of the earth.

Gather your supplies:

- Bowl
- Small rocks
- Pebbles
- Sand
- Dirt
- Water
- Mason jar
- Mason jar lid

In a bowl, mix your dirt, sand, and rocks together.

Fill your jar with this mixture.

Fill the jar up with water and put on the lid.

Set the jar in an out-of-the-way location. Observe the jar over a period of several days.

Over time, the ingredients in the jar will settle into distinct layers.

The Science

When there is heavy rain or other weather, rocks and soil move and erode. Erosion is the process of wind, water, or other natural forces breaking down soil and large rocks into tiny pieces of dirt and sand.

This dirt and sand mixture is called sediment. Wind and water carries sediment across the surface of the globe.

Eventually, sediment settles somewhere. Over time, more and more sediment is deposited at a location and hardens. Over thousands and millions of years, sediment is compressed into rocks.

But each layer of sediment is slightly different. So, when rocks are cut open, you can see the distinct layers (called strata) of sediment inside the rock.

Geologists use sediment layers to date fossils and determine how old an area of the world is. This is known as relative dating.

Questions to Ask

How long would it take for your jar to turn into a rock?

What can geologist learn from what is hiding inside rock formations?

How is relative dating important to learning more about the earth?

STEAM Extensions

Science: Learn about the basics of relative dating through rock layers. Visit a local rock formation. What can you tell about the rock using relative dating clues?

Technology: What other tools do scientists use to determine how old something is?

Engineering: How is knowing what's in a sediment layer important for engineers? How does an engineer use information about rocks when planning buildings, bridges, and roads?

Art: Make a collage of sediment layers using real sand, dirt, and gravel.

Math: Learn about the rock layers near your house. Can you use relative dating clues to determine how long people have populated your location?

SECTION 4: LIGHT, SOUND, AND MATTER

What is matter?

What is light?

Why does sound exist?

These questions have stumped scientists for thousands of years. Today, we know a lot about light, matter, and sound, but there is still a lot to learn.

These questions are so large that there is a branch of science devoted to answering them. This branch of science is called physics.

A physicist is a scientist who studies matter and energy through time, space, and the universe.

Because we are still learning about our universe, many questions that a physicist studies are theoretical, meaning they can't be proven yet. But many physics questions have been answered.

Learn more about sound, light, density, and surface tension in these science experiments.

HOW DOES SOUND WORK?

Someone claps and you hear it. Your mom or dad talks, and you can understand them.

But have you ever wondered how you're able to hear sounds? A doll has ears just like yours, but it is not able to process information and sound the way you can.

Try this experiment to learn about sound and how your ears translate vibrations into data you can understand.

Gather your supplies:

- Balloon
- Mason jar
- Salt
- Scissors

Cut the neck off your balloon with scissors and slip it over the top of your mason jar. Stretch the balloon tightly like a drum.

Sprinkle the top of your jar with salt.

Place your jar on a table and move your head close to it.

Hum a constant low note close to the jar. Take care not to blow the salt off the jar with your breath.

Watch as the salt jumps and dances in response to the sound coming from your mouth.

The Science

Sound is a vibration of matter that travels in waves through the air and through some materials.

In space, where molecules are very far apart from each other, you cannot hear sound. But on earth, where molecules are close together, sound can travel even across great distances.

Inside your ear, you have bones that capture sound vibrations. Inside your ear is something called a cochlea, which holds thousands of tiny hairs. These hairs capture the vibrations of sound, which transfers the signal to your brain, which then interprets the sound and lets you know what you are hearing.

The salt on the surface of the balloon moves in response to the sound waves you made when you hummed.

Questions to Ask

Do high or low sounds make bigger waves?

Why can we feel sound sometimes?

What is the quietest sound you can hear?

STEAM Extensions

Science: How fast do sound waves travel? What can make sound travel faster or slower?

Technology: Make a tin can phone. Attach a string between the bottom of two cans. Stretch the string tightly and speak into the can. Have a friend listen to the other can. The sound waves travel across the string and you can hear the voice clearly. This technology is how landline phones were invented.

Engineering: Acoustics are the engineering of sound. How did ancient engineers get sound to travel clearly without the use of microphones?

Art: Make a picture using sound wave patterns.

Math: Research the sound frequencies that different animals can hear. What is the frequency range that humans can hear?

HOW DO WE SEE?

You look at things every day, but have you ever thought about how your eyes actually see?

Our eyes are amazing pieces of biology that allow us to take in colors, shapes, and lights and turn them into patterns and objects that make sense to us. Eyes use a process called refraction to bend the light we see into objects that make sense to us.

You can see how this works first hand with this fun experiment.

Gather your supplies:

- Mason jar
- Water
- Colored markers
- Paper

Fill your mason jar with water.

Use the markers to draw a horizontal row of colors in a rainbow on your paper.

On another piece of paper, write the word STAR.

Place each paper behind the mason jar and look at it through the jar.

Move your head around the jar until you can get the rainbow to flip. You'll be able to tell it's flipped because the blue side of the rainbow will now be on the opposite side!

The word STAR flips to become the word RATS, only the letters backwards, too!

The Science

Eyes work by perceiving light. Light rays pass through the lens of your eyes and travel to the back of your eye, called the retina. The retina then sends the image to your brain—but the image it sends is upside down!

As light travels through a lens, it bends (or refracts), which can flip and warp the image. In this experiment, the mason jar is

the lens. When you move the paper behind the jar, you can watch the picture flip, but it's not magic, it's just light refraction!

Your eyes first see images upside down, just like they are in the mason jar. But your brain quickly turns them right side up.

Questions to Ask

What happens if you wear upside down glasses for a long time? Can your brain eventually double-flip the image to make you see correctly?

If our eyes were shaped differently, would they still work the same way?

Do animals' eyes work differently?

STEAM Extensions

Science: What other parts of the eye do we use to see?

Technology: Research the history of cameras. How did the first camera work? Can you make your own version at home?

Engineering: Build a 3D model of the eye.

Art: Paint a picture while squinting. Does this make it harder or easier to paint?

Math: How does the angle of light passing through a lens change how it comes out on the other side?

WHAT IS DENSITY?

Say you have two boxes that are the same size. One is filled with leaves. The other is filled with sand. Which is harder to pick up?

Even though both boxes are full, the box with the sand weighs a lot more because sand is a lot denser than leaves.

Every object in the world has a density rating. You can learn about the density of common kitchen liquids in this science experiment.

Gather your supplies:

- Mason jar
- Clear corn syrup
- Food coloring
- Blue dish soap
- Water
- Vegetable oil
- Rubbing alcohol

Pour 1/3 cup of clear corn syrup into the bottom of the jar. Color it purple with food coloring.

Carefully pour 1/3 cup of blue dish soap over the purple corn syrup.

Dye 1/3 of a cup of water green and pour it over the soap.

Pour 1/3 cup of vegetable oil over the water.

Dye 1/3 cup of rubbing alcohol red. Gently pour it over the surface of the oil.

The Science

Although they are all liquids, each of the liquids in this experiment have a different density. Corn syrup is the densest liquid, and rubbing alcohol is the least dense. By coloring them and stacking them, you can see their natural density, although normally it is difficult to see.

Questions to Ask

Where do other household liquids fit in the density column?

If you shake up the jar, will the ingredients separate again, or mix?

How is learning about density important for science?

STEAM Extensions

Science: Research the density of liquids. What is the densest liquid on earth? What is the least dense?

Technology: What happens when you take liquid into space? Does it retain the same density?

Engineering: Why is the density of liquid important for creating boats, spaceships, and planes?

Art: What other themes can you create for your density jar? Can you make an ocean-themed jar? What about a space-themed jar?

Math: The mathematical formula for density is mass divided by volume. In the science classroom, a triple beam balance scale can be used to measure mass. But at home, you can settle for measuring the weight on a kitchen or bathroom scale. Use this formula to find the density of common household objects: $D = m/V$

WHY DON'T ALL OBJECTS SINK?

When you toss an apple into a tub of water, does it float or sink? What about a rock?

What about a human?

Why are you more likely to sink without a life jacket than with one?

The secret lies in an object's buoyancy.

Conduct this quick science experiment to learn more about how buoyancy works.

Gather your supplies:

- 2 mason jars
- Water
- 2 tangerines

Fill your jars with water.

Place a tangerine in one of the jars. It will float.

Peel the other tangerine and place it inside the other jar. It sinks right to the bottom!

The Science

An object's buoyancy determines if it will float or sink in a liquid. The ancient Greek scientist Archimedes created a formula for buoyancy, known as Archimedes' Principle.

This principle states that if there is enough force pulling up on the object at the same rate at which the object is pulled through the liquid by gravity, then the object will float. In easier terms, it just means that if there is enough air or gas pulling on the object, it will float.

Tangerines have loose skin that holds a lot of air. This prevents the tangerines from sinking when they have the peel on. But when you take off the peel, the air is no longer trapped around the tangerine, so it sinks to the bottom.

Questions to Ask

Will removing the peel of other fruits or vegetables change whether they sink or float?

Why do some tangerines sink even with the peel on?

Can you tell how buoyant an object is by looking at it?

STEAM Extensions

Science: Try this experiment in other liquids. Does that change the results?

Technology: Design a life jacket for your peeled orange. Can you get it to float again?

Engineering: What everyday items rely on buoyancy to work?

Art: Draw a picture of the tangerine's buoyancy in the water before and after peeling.

Math: Research the mathematical formula for buoyancy. How is this formula used in the real world?

WHAT IS PITCH?

You may have seen videos of women and men (or even kids) filling glasses with water and playing some of your favorite songs by rubbing the top of the glasses. Maybe you've even tried it yourself!

But have you ever wondered why adding different amounts of water to a glass can make different sounds?

The secret is in a scientific principle known as pitch. Learn more about pitch in this fun experiment!

Gather your supplies:

- 7 mason jars
- Wooden skewers or metal utensils
- Water
- Food coloring

Tap your empty jars with your sticks to hear the base pitch.

Fill your jars with varying levels of water. Add a splash of food coloring to each to make a rainbow.

Tap the sticks on the jars. The sound that each jar makes is different! The pitch has changed.

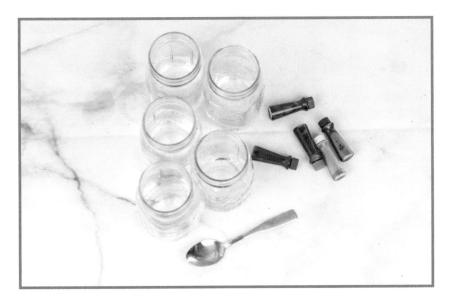

The Science

The empty jars all make the same sound. This is because the sound waves all travel the same in objects that are shaped the same.

Pro tip: If you want to get fancy, play sound clips of a major musical scale. See if you can get your jars to make those same notes!

But when you add water, the way the sound waves travel is changed. The more water you add to a jar, the lower the pitch. Adding varying levels of water to jars will make a variety of pitches that you can use to make music.

Questions to Ask

Why are some notes pleasant while others are unpleasant?

How many different pitches can you make with your jars?

Can you play *Mary Had a Little Lamb* with your jars?

STEAM Extensions

Science: The most famous musical scale is the diatonic scale. This scale contains the notes, C, D, E, F, G, A, B. Why is this scale universally pleasing?

Technology: How are science and music linked? What technologies are used in music today?

Engineering: Build an original instrument from things you have lying around at home.

Art: Compose an original song on your water xylophone.

Math: Music follows the same principles as math. Counting, rhythm, pitch, harmonies, intervals, and patterns are all present in math and music. How would music sound different if it didn't follow distinct mathematical principles?

WHAT IS SURFACE TENSION?

If you've visited a pond, you may have seen tiny little insects and beetles glide across the water like it's ice. You may have even tried gliding on the surface of water yourself, ending up a soggy mess.

Have you ever wondered why insects can glide across the surface of the water, but you can't?

It's all due to surface tension.

Learn a bit more about surface tension in this fun experiment.

Watch out! You'll need a parent or other adult helper for this project.

Gather your supplies:

- Hardboiled egg
- Candle
- Lighter
- Mason jar
- Water
- Tongs

Pro tip: Be careful when handling the sooty egg. If you rub the soot off the egg, the experiment won't work.

Have an adult hard boil the egg. When the egg is completely cool, have an adult light your candle.

Fill your mason jar with water.

Use tongs to hold the egg over the flames. This will apply a thin coating of soot over the egg and turn it black.

When the egg is all black, carefully drop it into the water.

Look closely—the egg has turned silver!

The Science

How does an egg turn from black to silver? The secret is surface tension and light refraction.

If you looked at the sooty egg under a microscope, you would see that soot is not smooth at all, but rough and jagged. To understand why the egg appears silver, you need to know about a few scientific principles.

Water molecules are made up of hydrogen and oxygen molecules. Water forms droplets because of hydrogen bonding. Hydrogen atoms would rather bond with other hydrogen atoms before bonding with other molecules, keeping like molecules together. So when water molecules are near each other, their hydrogen molecules form a gentle bond together that keeps the water molecules in one spot. This gentle bond that forms creates surface tension, which resists external forces.

A hydrophobic molecule is a molecule that does not want to bond with a water molecule. Carbon is a hydrophobic molecule, and soot contains a large amount of carbon.

When the sooty egg is dropped into the water, the water never touches the egg. The soot pushes back against the water, creating a barrier of air all around the egg that stays in place because of surface tension. When you look at the egg in the water, you're seeing the light reflected back from the water surrounding the egg, not the egg itself. This gives the illusion that the egg has turned silver, even though it's completely covered in black soot.

Questions to Ask

Could we survive without surface tension?

Where do you see surface tension every day?

Is surface tension ever harmful?

STEAM Extensions

Science: Try this other fun surface tension experiment: Fill a bowl with water. Sprinkle pepper on the water. Add a drop of dish soap onto the water. Watch as the pepper quickly flies to the edges of the bowl.

Technology: How would the world be different if there was no surface tension?

Engineering: Chemical engineers use the properties of surface tension to create surfaces and fabrics that repel water. Try making your own water-repellant fabric.

Art: Take a picture of your silver egg and share it with friends and family!

Math: The mathematical formula for surface tension calculates the amount of energy required to increase the surface area of a liquid (or how much force is required to spread the liquid). What force do you have to apply to a small puddle of liquid to get it to change shape?

SECTION 5: EARTH AND SPACE SCIENCE

How much do you know about our world?

Why does the earth have layers?

How far away are the planets?

What makes rocks look the way they do?

How are planets formed?

These are the questions that astronomers and geologists ask and answer every day.

But you don't have to be an adult to learn more about the stars, planets, and the world around us. These simple earth and space science experiments can answer your biggest questions about space, gravity, and what makes up our world.

HOW BIG IS THE SOLAR SYSTEM?

The solar system is big. Really big.

But do you know how big?

If the sun were 12 inches in diameter, Jupiter would be just 1.2 inches in diameter, and Pluto would be a tiny .02 inches in diameter.

Try this simple experiment to find out the scale of our solar system.

Gather your supplies:

- Air dry clay
- Toothpicks
- Waterproof glue
- Fishing line
- Mason jar lid
- Mason jar
- Water
- Glitter
- Dish soap
- Ruler

Use the following scale to make your planets:

- Jupiter 120%
- Saturn 100%
- Uranus 45%
- Neptune 40%
- Earth 11%
- Venus 10%
- Mars 5%
- Mercury 4%
- Pluto 2%

Use air dry clay to form your planets. Work your way from largest to smallest for greater accuracy. Make Saturn 1 inch in diameter and use the ruler to approximate the size scale for the rest of the planets.

Use the following color scheme:

Jupiter: Brown with white streaks
Saturn: Yellow with a white ring
Uranus: Blue
Neptune: Blue with white stripes
Earth: Green, blue, and white
Venus: Orange with brown streaks
Mars: Red
Mercury: Orange
Pluto: Blue and white

Poke a small hole into the top of each planet with a toothpick. Leave the toothpicks in place as the clay dries overnight.

The next morning, remove the toothpicks and glue a piece of fishing line inside each hole. Let the glue dry 2 hours.

Glue the other side of the fishing line to your mason jar lid. Let the glue dry 24 hours.

Once the glue dries, fill your jar with water and add a few sprinkles of glitter. Add a tiny drop of dish soap to disperse the glitter throughout the jar.

Carefully place the lid onto the jar and close it tightly.

Flip the jar upside down. The planets will try to rise to the top of the jar, suspending them in the center of the jar.

Pro tip: When arranging your planets, space them carefully on the lid or they will get tangled when you flip the jar.

The Science

Planets are huge. But since planets look so tiny in the sky, we often forget how big they really are. This activity helps show the scale of the solar system planets in relation to one another.

Using this scale, the sun would be just about the size of a beach ball. There's no way that's fitting into a mason jar!

Questions to Ask

Why are the planets as big as they are?

Do you think Earth is the only planet that can sustain life?

How many miles apart are the planets in the solar system?

STEAM Extensions

Science: Remember that the sun is about the same size as a beach ball compared to these planets. Paint a beach ball orange and place it near the jar to display the full scale of the solar system.

Technology: Examine the night sky using a telescope. How many of the planets can you find?

Engineering: How do aerospace engineers use the facts about the solar system when determining how to design space craft?

Art: Add a bit of food coloring to the liquid in the jar to make it look more like space.

Math: Research the scale of how far away planets are from one another. If one mile equals one inch, how far would you have to walk to get to the other side of the solar system?

HOW DO ORBITS WORK?

Have you ever wondered why planets orbit around the sun? What is an orbit, anyway?

An orbit is the path of a planet, moon, or object around a larger object with a greater gravitational pull. The sun has a large mass (332,946 times greater than the Earth), which pulls all the planets toward it.

Planets also each have their own gravitational pull, which prevents them from crashing into the sun. But depending on where the planet is in its orbit, it will be closer or farther from the sun.

When the Earth is close to the sun, it is hotter on Earth. When the Earth is farther away from the sun, it is colder on Earth. Each complete orbit of the Earth around the sun takes one year. The orbit of the Earth around the sun causes the seasons to change on Earth.

You can test how orbits work using a mason jar, fishing wire, and a metal washer.

Gather your supplies:

- Mason jar
- Metal washer

- Fishing line
- Scissors
- Tape

Turn your mason jar upside down under a cabinet hanging over a countertop in your kitchen. You can also do this experiment under a table.

Cut a piece of fishing line long enough to reach from the bottom of the cabinet to just below the top of the jar.

Tie a metal washer to one end of the string.

Tape the other end of the string to the bottom of the cabinet or table, directly above the jar. The washer will rest against the jar.

Push the washer away from the jar, parallel to the jar. The washer will swing around the jar several times before coming back to rest against the side of the jar.

The Science

Every object has a gravitational pull. This is the pull of the object's mass. Since the mass of the jar is bigger than that of the washer, the washer is pulled into the jar. But, the mass of the washer keeps the washer from flying directly into the jar. This creates an oval-shaped orbit like that of planets, comets, and satellites.

The momentum of the object also affects its orbit. When you push the washer at the right speed, it goes into orbit, but if you push it too soft or too hard, it either crashes directly into the jar or never starts the orbit.

Questions to Answer

What is gravity?

What is momentum?

What is mass?

What happens when you push the washer so it's moving quickly?

What happens when you push it so it's moving slowly?

STEAM Extensions

Science: See if you can get other objects to orbit the jar.

Technology: Record your orbit on video and watch it in slow-motion.

Engineering: Change how fast you push the washer. Try using a bigger or smaller jar and see if that affects the orbit.

Art: Put a piece of paper under the washer and jar, and a dab of paint on the washer. As the washer orbits the jar, the orbit's shape will drip onto the paper below.

Math: Calculate how many times the washer will orbit the jar when pushed in different directions and at different speeds.

HOW ARE CRYSTALS FORMED?

Crystals are amazing. Natural crystals are formed using ionic bonds, which is a type of molecular bonding that repeats the same pattern over and over.

Crystals are everywhere in our world. Salt, snowflakes, ice, and gemstones are all types of crystals.

You can make your very own crystal garden at home using monoammonium phosphate powder.

Gather your supplies:

- Water
- Monoammonium phosphate powder
- Food coloring
- Mason jar
- Clear glue
- Paintbrush

Get an adult to help you boil a ½ cup of water on the stove. Add six tablespoons of monoammonium phosphate powder to the water and stir until dissolved.

Add your desired color of food coloring.

Coat the inside of your jar with glue. Sprinkle fresh monoammonium phosphate powder onto the glue and shake the jar gently to coat it with the powder.

Fill the jar with the water.

Place the jar in a safe location and wait 3 days. You'll know the crystals are ready when the water above the crystals turns clear.

Pour out any remaining water.

Examine the crystals left behind.

The Science

The crystal powder inside the water is called a solute. The crystal molecules bounce around in the solvent (the water) and start sticking together through ionic bonding. Ionic bonds are not flexible, and form a specific shape

depending on the type of molecules. Over time, a crystal structure starts to form. This process is called nucleation.

Questions to Ask

What does the chemical structure of monoammonium phosphate crystals look like?

Does adding more water or more crystal powder change how the crystals look?

Why are some chemical bonds ionic, and some covalent (flexible)?

STEAM Extensions

Science: What other types of crystals can you make at home? Try making crystals from Epsom salt, table salt, and borax.

Technology: Examine the shape of the crystals with a magnifying glass or microscope. Can you see the repeating pattern?

Engineering: Does adding things to the jar change how the crystals react?

Art: Experiment with making crystals from different colors. Which color makes the prettiest crystals?

Math: How long does it take for crystals to grow? Does changing the amount of crystal powder change how long it takes for the crystals to form?

WHAT MAKES ROCKS GLOW IN THE DARK?

Have you ever visited a rock exhibit at a museum? Under a black light, some rocks glow in the dark! These rocks are fluorescent, because they glow under a black light. Rocks that glow in the dark are phosphorescent because they emit their own light.

A rock that is fluorescent temporarily absorbs light, then releases the light back on a different wavelength. This makes the rock appear to be a different color, and is fascinating to observe!

Gather your supplies:

- Fluorescent rocks
- Mason jar
- Soil
- Black light flashlight

Fill your jar about halfway with soil.

Arrange your rocks inside the jar to showcase their most fluorescent sides.

Take the rock garden into a dark room. Shine the black light onto the rocks to reveal their hidden colors.

The Science

Some fluorescent rocks are reflective with shortwave UV light, while others only glow under longwave UV light. Shortwave UV light is dangerous, as it can cause radiation damage to the skin or eyes. Black light flashlights use longwave UV light, which is safe for the skin.

Rocks that glow under a longwave UV light include:

- Calcite
- Tugtupite
- Adamite
- Sphalerite
- Fluorite
- Scheelite

Look for mineral sets that contain these rocks when selecting your minerals.

Fluorescent minerals contain chemicals that react with the UV rays in a black light. The chemicals in the rocks reflect the light back from the UV light along a different wavelength, making the rock look like it's suddenly a different color.

Questions to Ask

Why do some rocks glow and others don't?

Would breaking the rock stop it from glowing?

Why don't the rocks glow under every kind of light?

STEAM Extensions

Science: Research the light spectrum. What types of light are there? What is the visible light spectrum?

Technology: Shine different types of light on the rocks. What happens when you shine a fluorescent light on the rocks? Does a black light bulb produce different effects than a black light flashlight?

Engineering: How would life be different if the only visible light was black light?

Art: If you have some rocks that don't glow, paint them with fluorescent paint so they will glow under the black light, too.

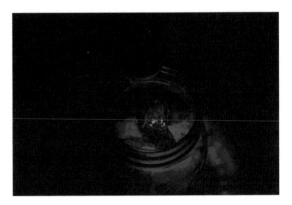

Math: What percentage of the light spectrum can we see with human eyes?

WHAT IS A NEBULA?

A nebula is a cloud of dust and gas in the space between stars.

When you look at a picture of space or through a telescope, there are sections that look cloudy and dusty. This section of space is known as a nebula. Sometimes these areas appear pink, purple, and bright blue.

You can make your own nebula following the directions below.

Gather your supplies:

- Cotton balls
- Mason jar
- Water
- Blue acrylic paint
- Purple acrylic paint
- Pink acrylic paint
- Glitter

Pull the cotton balls apart so that they look wispy.

Fill 1/3 of the jar full of water. Squeeze two tablespoons of blue paint into the water. Add a sprinkle of glitter. Close the lid and shake up the jar.

Drop cotton balls into the jar until they absorb all the water.

Fill another third of the jar with water, this time adding two tablespoons of purple paint. Add a sprinkle of glitter. Close the lid and shake.

Pro tip: The brighter your paint, the brighter your nebula will look. Look for neon paints at your local craft store.

Add another layer of cotton balls to soak up the water.

Repeat the process one final time with pink paint.

The Science

A nebula is more than just dust. Most nebulae contain bits of dust, helium gas, plasma, and hydrogen. A nebula is often the birthplace of new stars. Nebulae are an important part of interstellar medium (the ingredients that make up space). Over time, gravity pulls the matter of space together, forming these nebulae clouds. When the clouds get bigger and pull together, they collapse into new stars and planets. Nebulae are like the parents of planets, solar systems, and stars.

Questions to Ask

How far away is the closest nebula?

How much matter is necessary to make new stars and plants?

How long does it take for a nebula to make a new star or planet?

STEAM Extensions

Science: What are the names of the closest nebulae?

Technology: Use a telescope to examine the sky at night. Can you see any nebulae?

Engineering: What would happen if nebulae had a higher or lower gravitational pull?

Art: Draw or paint your own nebula.

Math: How far away is the nearest nebula? How long would it take to get there in a spaceship? How long would it take in a plane?

WHAT ARE CONSTELLATIONS?

Constellations have fascinated humans for thousands of years. But did you know that constellations don't really exist?

There is nothing in space that connects certain stars together. Humans invented the constellations to track time, distance, and directions. The invention of constellations helped lead to other big inventions, including astronomy, ocean travel, and space travel. So even though constellations aren't "real," they are a huge part of our science and technology systems today.

You can make your own model of constellations following the directions below.

Gather your supplies:

- Mason jar
- Blue acrylic paint
- Glow-in-the-dark acrylic paint
- Paintbrush
- Acrylic sealer
- Black permanent marker

Paint your jar with blue paint and let dry. You may need to apply 2-3 coats of paint.

Find a picture of constellations in a book or online.

Trace the lines of the constellations onto your jar using your permanent marker.

Add a dot of glow-in-the-dark paint to make the stars in each constellation. Let the paint dry.

Spray the entire jar with acrylic sealer to prevent the paint from chipping. Let dry for 24-48 hours, following the directions on your sealer.

Place your jar in a dark room and turn out the lights. Watch as your constellations come to life.

Questions to Ask

Why aren't the constellations always visible?

What are the names of the stars in your constellations?

How many miles away are the constellations?

How long would it take to travel to the constellations?

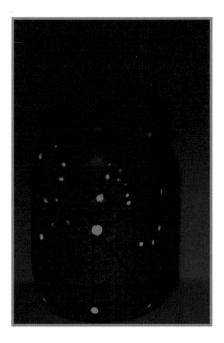

STEAM Extensions

Science: How do scientists and astronauts use constellations?

Technology: Research what constellations are visible in the spring, summer, winter, and fall in your area. Paint each season's constellations onto a different side of your jar or make one jar for each season.

Engineering: Visit a local planetarium. What engineering techniques are used to mimic the appearance of the night sky? How could the planetarium become even more immersive?

Art: Use different colors of glow-in-the-dark paint for your stars.

Math: Find out the distance between the constellations. How far are they from earth?

SUPPLEMENTS

Use these worksheets when completing your science experiments to take your learning to the next level.

Directions for use:

Scan the worksheets into your computer. Print as many copies as you need for each experiment. You can also download each worksheet at themasonjarscientist.com.

For additional resources, visit themasonjarscientist.com and download the complete STEM extension pack!

STEM extension worksheet

Name:_____

What are you testing?

Draw your results

STEAM elements used:

SCIENCE:

TECHNOLOGY:

ENGINEERING:

ART:

MATH:

Science experiment worksheet

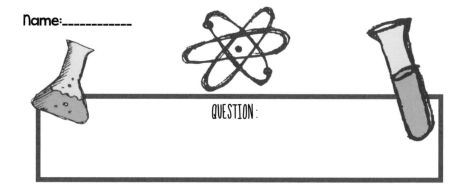

Name:_____

QUESTION :

HYPOTHESIS :

EXPERIMENT :

CONTROL :

VARIABLE 1 :

VARIABLE 2 :

VARIABLE 3 :

VARIABLE 4 :

INDEX